Book : Insoc

Natural robotics and intelligence design

By Bastiaan Oostendorp

© 2017 Lulu Bastiaan Oostendorp . Alle Rechten Voorbehouden.
ISBN 978-1-326-93096-7

# Table of Contents

Table of Contents ................................................................ 3
material source of life ....................................................... 6
mind of knowledge ........................................................... 7
Martial Observation unit .................................................... 8
Usage for natural elements .............................................. 10
Limited science ................................................................ 11
Expected Outcome ........................................................... 12
Protocol ........................................................................... 13
Observation rules ............................................................. 14
mathematics .................................................................... 16
space time fabric ............................................................. 18
architecture of past-sentience ........................................ 19
Communication Antenna ................................................. 21
Light Frequency ............................................................... 22
Nano Core ........................................................................ 25
Photonic power source ................................................... 27
VCU voice control unit .................................................... 29
Aiding robotics ................................................................ 30
computer takeover. ......................................................... 31
value of information and money .................................... 34
Bites of action ................................................................. 36

Leaps of revolution ................................................................... 37

important priority ..................................................................... 39

Sentry-Grid ................................................................................ 41

Computer Aided Intelligence ................................................... 43

Learning Artifical Unit .............................................................. 44

Crippling nano .......................................................................... 46

Restricting Areas ....................................................................... 47

pattern seeking ......................................................................... 48

Emergency Handle .................................................................... 50

generic symbolic comprehension ............................................ 51

recumberance ........................................................................... 52

costs of instrumental creation ................................................. 53

priority layers ............................................................................ 54

vision regent ............................................................................. 56

Transition .................................................................................. 58

Police Grid ................................................................................. 60

Data Museum ............................................................................ 61

Nano – bots ............................................................................... 62

Automatic defense unit ............................................................ 63

Terminator 2.3 .......................................................................... 64

Storage element ....................................................................... 65

Artificial Intelligent symbol communication .......................... 67

Visible Cognition ............................................................. 68

list of possibilities ........................................................... 70

Reaction schemes .......................................................... 71

formulas of emotion ...................................................... 72

Isaac Asimov ................................................................... 74

Smart Picture Mind picture ............................................ 75

Ethical issues .................................................................. 77

Reasons of design ........................................................... 79

## material source of life

The animals and humans have corresponding parts in their bodies.
An animal has behaviour to keep alife.
From foodsearching, protection of territory, to communication with fellow animals.
The humans have a body and intelligent behaviour to keep alife too.
The humans all share a body with identical parts(identical functions of body-parts)
The way humans look can differ but all have a torso, legs, arms, head.
When we would step in the feet of the creator we would see that animals have bodyparts similar to ours.
That plants named after how they look have resemblance to parts of our bodies.
For example a walnut has inside the form of our brains.
the source materials of all living beings are shared by all individuals, but functions are less or more advanced.
A monkey can communicate and is by body more looking like a human but is less able to have intelligent behaviour.
The creator did create all living beings, and used a large amount of different parts not having any living being being unique.
The creator choose from basic forms, and drew the species to have the broad range of what exists.
The material source of life, is not unique, but a choice of the creator forming all living beings like a program containing a set of rules or algorithms.

## mind of knowledge

In the far past as is written in the bible, book genesis there was mankind, adam and eve which were in the paradise on earth.
The adam and eve were happy and lived a content life.
But when they ate from that one tree which they were forbidden to do they fell into sadness.
The tree from which they ate was not a normal tree it was a symbol for what it was known for.
It induced the mind function in their living experience.
The human was born with a mind giving them grief in their lives.
The mind which was described by jesus as those poor in mind are on the path to heaven.
The mind which was in the bible described as, from a living soul to a creating life by intellect.
The mind of knowledge is an instrument that works for an abstract appearance.
In the future we will be able to load the mind of someone with information, not just by viewing it or reading it as we study today,
but by sending it like a computercommunication device into their brains into their minds.
It is a way of making humans a level higher in ways to cope with life.
In the days to come, every child is impregnated with the knowledge and expertise it needs for his function on our world.
A day to come, that learning is not anymore making exercises to train experience, but a choice of connecting a computer to transfer knowledge.

## Martial Observation unit

The newspapers sometimes give news to what terrorist attacks are done.
Attacks on important buildings, having casualties and victims.
The newspapers give the argument that our world is slowly degrading to a battle for strong values.
Where people strong and dangerous have the right on their name.
But the terrorist attacks can not be solved by more dange, more violence.
In the high ranks there is a discovery being tested and prepared and that
is named Martial observation unit.
It is a small orb, the size of a tennis-ball. It is neutral in color and is not seen when active.
It floats a couple of meters above ground (10 to 100 meters)
It is capable of recording visual data and sound data.
It has an artifical unit to make it float in logical ways above the normal area's (industry, housing, important areas)
The artificial unit is comparable to the ones in scientific fields being used for new purposes.
(a unit similar to the ones used in quadracopters)
The theory is that in the future when a large terrorist attack is made, these form of surveillance is being used to counter attack the terrorists.
The orbs because they flow not directly in our sight are most of the time not seen by our human eyes.
When the world will be placed under martial law, this is one of the instruments they use for controlling the crowd, for controlling terrorists.

Martial law is an answer to violence, uncontrolled violence. But the normal person has no right on the streets to have privacy.
When such a observation rule is activated its a deprivation of our society because it can be used for bad purposes also.
A despot or saprat can use it to enslave people, because controll can be expressed in many ways yet unknown.

## Usage for natural elements

The computer and robotic industry focusses on using mineral substance to make objects capable of simple behaviour.
simple because it is sometimes logic, sometimes mathamtics to calculate or base behaviour.
robotics made of metal or plastic.
computers made of chips made of silicate.
In the near future we will step towards a new field of discovery.
It will be called natural elements.
It will put inside a translation pod.
The translation pod translating natural impulses, glucose based, oxygen based, and electrical circuits.
The pod is attached to a natural element.
An element that is part of a natural living being, for example a spider.
The spider being prepared is cut off from his body, legs, eyes, and coupled to a pod.
a translation pod able to read the impulses of the spider and putting it to what is necesary for that robot or computer.
In a future a little bit further the socalled robots can be coupled to our brain, giving us input from it, enhancing our memory and intelligence functions.
The only problem is that the longer we are attached to a certain device containing a natural element, the more there are unknown influences not prevented.
Influences in character or memory bias.
When such a device is coupled to our brain, it has not a big form. it is as small as an usb stick.

# Limited science

As our human race we have a past, a history in which we are known for the primitive part.
In medieval and before we did not have computers, machines and all luxerious we have today.
In the far past we were as good and modern as we are today, but because of misbehaving we got punished.
The punishment that our science was destroyed.
The punishment to be casted back to medieval technology and civilisation.
Our human race has been as good as it is now and even beyond our current status of science and scientific technology.
In those times a subgroup of our humanrace, which was ordered to safe us for long times, built a device, or a group of devices giving us teh security that such misbehaviour would never ever appear anymore.
Those devices, still working, are invisible to us.
Some say thay float below clouds, others say they are buried in the antartic fields.
The devices scan for certain emitted radiation and then erase the memory of the inventors. Giving them the idea their discovery was not succesfull.
The devices, they would read and alter our minds. Because that is a sort of antenna for being intellectual and logical.
The devices, no one know their names anymore. And no one can operate them.
They are there to safeguard our race for the biggest evils we not know.

## Expected Outcome

In biology we know a certain theory named the black box.
In biology it is not important how a decision is made by animals,
but what decision was the source of an observed action.
A black box creating actions of animals.
A black box, resulting in animals of doing this to get food, doing that to defend a territory.
In robotics a certain artificial intelligent design is not measured by how its working or what counts as the source of result.
But the action as being perceived by us.
When an animal learns to eat, fight, mate. we measure it by what is does.
In similar ways we could build a robot with a backend of artificial intelligence.
In a way we would not understand how the computer works or how it learns.
We would judge the robot by what it does in several situation or preconfigured actions.
The expected outcome would we a set of figured situation.
A place with a certain test. and us wanting a robot which is able to solve it.
If the robot solves it, and not only once but when it is presented.
the robot has a value on expected outcome.
With how efficient or effective it is etc.
The expected outcome as a measure how robotics are effective and to be able to compare them.

# Protocol

The computer-science from the beginning went from improvisation and creativity to a way of controlling all devices by parts governed by protocols.
By protocols we use computers with windows, unix or apple.
By protocols we browse the internet and are able to read all sites we search for.
The first computers were primitive but the source of our current-day technologies.
A protocol is a set of conditions making able that companies can inter-relate with their made products with those of others.
A protocol also gives the consumer the safety of buying something with main features that are prooved working.
With computers it costed a couple of years. We expect that with robotics. Untill the time there are humanoids who are able to operate it will cost also a couple of years.

## Observation rules

When we would build a robot capable of recognizing what it sees.
In what way would we have to store the interpretation of the view.
We want to prevent that when one element changes it is not recognized anymore at all.
A certain structure of describing is needed.
When a robot would be in an environnement of normal humans it would need a similar way of describing as do humans have.
For example we could describe every object or process we see.
Or for example we would make an intelligent system that gives numbers and ranges to objects making it a big whole of numbers.
The last thing is that when we wold not anymore understand which number is pointing to which object or part of object.
For a robot, abstractly said we need a symbollanguage which is convertable into other kinds of robots.
A symbolic language being able to describe at different levels and layers.
A very concrete way, how does something look, color, size, form.
A more abstract way, what is the intention of the object and when its a life-creature is it healthy, broken, needing something.
A abstract way, what is the purpose of the robot himself, and what goals are there in the given environnement.
All parts of a symbolic language needed for robots to be able to interact with a given situation.
When one element would change in that situation, you want the robot to keep acting as is predetermined.

The concrete description can be almost like a vector file with textures of photographic style.
A process you can describe as a logical way. making an object, a subject, a process holding interaction, giving each object an intention or goal.
A third layer the wanted interaction for the robot with reality checks if its able or avaiable to do that.
And a fourth layer which judges it all on its moral value.
Observation is something that is important for every life creature, so will it be for robots too.
If observation is invalid, the more power a creature has, the more it can destroy.
A robot capable of nuclear weapons, you do not want to make a false judgment, inducing a nuclear war.

## mathematics

In computer language the elementral stone is the binary range of numbers.
One binary zero or one describes the value of a number.
When a number reaches a certain point, with a large amount of precisity.
A number having more than 10 digits with a floating point in it.
In a metaphysical stage a number represents a information element.
A number in itself doesn't mean much, but it describes a quality into a quantity.
A number is describable an adress.
In a simple form the housenumber in a street, the postal code, the identifier of a telephone.
A number is a symbol that is not dependent on words or elements describing an object.
A number is a symbol which is given a position in an amount or range that counts a certain weight.
When language meets the computer, words are meaningless because a computer has no idea of it what it is.
When numbers meet a computer it can do mathetic and geomatric counts.
The invention of using numbers has been appearant from four thousands years ago.
But the computer less then five decades ago.
We could not predic onecentury ago that computers would relief us.
Language can grow from something only for the happy few to a worldwide medium to spread information like lifestories, expertise and communication.

This tells us that in the future we can expect to use language en mathematic in a more advanced way we now cannot think of.
A new numerical system is to have digits value the place in a number or amount.
In our static numerical way it is tenfold every place in a number.
When we count from one to 100 we count the first 10 on the first digit, and the next digit we count the decimal numbers.
A numerical system is to let every digit count from the former digit to the quadrated digit on the next.
In this way large numbers are being counted with the smalles kind of number of digitized range.
This numerical system only works when there is no precision needed but a comparison between ranges.
This is an idea, not a proven theory. I might sound a bit unlogical.
It is as looking in the blind to create something not known.
If you have a number that way, every digit a quadrate of the last. a precision is made by the opposite,
making the same number, same range of digits by making them the square root.

## space time fabric

Einstein had the theory of relativity.
A theory explaining when time is interacting with space.
His theory was there is one continuum.
One continuum of space multiplied by time.
When both collide it is functioning as it is one part and whole.
The space matter holds all the objects which are visible in it.
The space matter gives all objects a place at which it is bound, unless
forces interact on it; giving it speed and motion.
Speed on how fast it travels from space during time.
And motion giving it a speed in time how fast time passes by in comparison to other time elements.
The space time fabric is the whole in universe that holds all objects in a time continuum we call always.
The time space can be altered at which if you remove a object with its root out of space it is accessable everywhere in space.
And if you remove an object with its root out of the time it is accessable anytime.
It sounds strange such a theory.
So when an object is disconnected from space, all motion does not apply to the object making it float on the space it is,
and accessable from any other space point.
It is a way of giving an object a temporal imagery position.
A fictive place can be used for unlimited features.
When such a theory would be with proof, there is the problem of how to use it.
Because it could be used with a variety of purposes not all being friendly.

## architecture of past-sentience

A time ago, before our christian timeline. Before it started at zero ac, after christ there was a civilisation,
We only have the rumors about trans-atlantis where a superior technlogy was used and gave prosperity to many.
The atlantic times where electricity was used even in advance of us.
A time when the people had lower moral standards and were subject to a final penitance, the destruction of their society by a so called angel.
As humans every force giving a change in society or doing things not seen as human intervention is calles to be angels-influence.
Atlantis was thrown into the ocean and wiped off the earth. But they had a vast amount of so called computer input and output.
When they were accessing computers they had not anymore as we own a silicate form that gives its data on a lcd screen.
They had a form of intelligence, aided by their computer technology directly attached to their brain.
The computersource they had was a ring around the earth. We look at it as a blue layer making sunlight appear through our eyes.
But it is far more advanced and is a layer being attached to a computerinvention wealready lost times ago.
It is said that guardians of humanity use it as their source for analytics, mathematica and logics.
The guardians use it to safeguard our reality, our world to invaders we not know of.

The guardians had a human form, but because of their link to such a big amount of sentient computer they have acces to all the technology, all the instruments we only can dream of.
The guardians of humanity.
We are not seeing them, we don't know them.
But when the time is right they will contact us.
Untill that time, atlantic-society will be a myth, a rumor.

## Communication Antenna

We know the seti program, giving a patternseeking algorithm the chance of finding intelligent communication in space.
The seti, compares content of a radio-telescope to all kinds of repatetive language like elements.
The seti, in that way is looking for life-forms able of communicating through mangetic sources.
But what is missing is the telescope not able to look very far.
A scope is a couple to a dozen meters big. so it is like looking through the hole of a pin to an object several meters away.
It is more effiecient to not use telesopes any more.
But finding away to use the earth. the planet as an antenna.
Because the earth is filled with dense metal and other ingredients it is a perfect antenna, if you want to catch certain communication.
An antenna made of our planet is also a way of communicating in both ways.
Not only listening but also sending.
Make it available for all of us,
to be part of an universe capable of communication
part of an interstellar society.
The planet is from metal, water, air and a shell of some kind.
If we use it wisely there is a vast possible uses for not only the ground under our feet.
But also the uses yet unknown, yet unkthinkable.

## Light Frequency

We alle know kight having its visible part and its invisible part.
Visible is the color. the color we like in paintings.
The color we like in our friendes and family.
Suppose the color would disappear and you would only see the outlines of what you look at.
For example your friend was first full colour, having color on his or her clothes, having color on shoes,
on hair color.
Suppose the color disappeared and you would only see around his body a little black line.
Would you still recognize him as your friend. Probably very difficult.
When light has a frequency we see it is a visible spectrum, or a part of visible appearance.
Now the light is another frequency. not visible to us.
We see nothing of the outtside frequencies of visibility.
When a creature has an appearance of light outside of the visible spectrum we would not see it.
But when we would touch that creature we would feel it is there. but we cannot see it.
Now suppose light is a medium that works as electrons. When it is part of a molecule it gives a form to something that was liquid or without form.
By the electrons it gets attached to fellow molecules.
When light would point at an object. it attacks the melecules or atoms it points at.
And the object raising a frequency in atoms shines back with the multiplier of the atom-structure and the lightwaves. (a wave of certain frequency, wavelength, wavestrenght,speed)

An atom reflects the light depending on the lightwave form and the kind of atom.
An atom. when receiving a black light wave, is not reflecting any light because the photons don't raise in the atom an energy-current giving it the visible color as perceived through the eye.
Now think of an object, a bird. The bird normally you see and recognize as a bird, and as the kind of bird.
Now shine on it with black light. It is not visible at all.
It is method of cloaking.
As the bird would be touched with white light it appears different as with orangje light.
This is the change in the lightwave that influences the appearance of what its pointing at.
Now the bird is surrounded with a atombase, similar as the blakc light.
It is reasonable that when in light there is black light, nonvisible, there should be material that is also black.
When a bird is surrounded like a shell by black mass. (black mass making invisible by reflection of material)
it disappears totally.
A nonvisible material can be used for a lot of things.
You can make certain things invisible.
When an atom, reflects light, it gives the color back.
When a light turns to black, it reflects on the object without casting a color back. Making it for camera's and life forms invisible to see.
When an atom turns to black, even with normal sunlight it is not visible.
Black mass. its one form of mass, of material.
Black mass also points to a material being the opposite of the elements in the chemical elements list. (atom based, weight value)

Black mass also points to a mass being opposed to all natural materials. making it a artificial material with part of bad side-effects not in natural materials

# Nano Core

Our planet holds things yet unknown.
Kind of creatures we never have seen before are hiding in places we did not enter.
Kind of creatures with forms we never imagined.
One creature, not only on our planet is a nano core.
It is the form of a globe. The same form as a planet.
The same form as a roud piece of fruit.
But the size is smaller. It is as big as a couple nanometers.
It is as big, no-one can see it when it is in plain sight.
IT is as big that when it moves, no-one sees it travelling.
It is called a nano-core. Because it is that small.
It is called a core because it is as solid as a rock or as solid as diamond.
The core has a part inside of it with, we would compare it with a computer made of life tissue.
The core has functionality to connect to a soul or spirit.
The core has functionality to communicate with that soul or spirit.
A core that travels and connects to a spirit.
For the intention of saving a soul,
For the intention of giving communication to a higher plan.
A nano-core. We don't see them, we are not aware of their existence.
But if they would exist. May they work together for the sake of intelligent life in this universe.
As when they are nano-cores and they are small they can travel far distances. they can travel arge distances without being detected.
These nano-cubes hold the knowledge of several races of intelligent life scattered through the universe.

The size of nanometers make them able to travel with the speed of light.
(understanding the theory of einstein, which says when an object is smaller, less gravitation or mass energy is needed for its speed and momentum thus able to travel faster)

## Photonic power source

We know the laser technology of giving light its path of straight line towards it pointing goal.
Its as tech used in range of objects from the laser pointing in a classroom on the wall with beamed information.
Its used in military as a weapon blinding opponents or pointing a target for a laser guided missile.
A laser is technology using a beam of photons towards it goal and giving multiplication by a semi transparent mirror and a piece of a transparant stone. (ruby)
When the photons in the beam are replicated making both a stronger beam and giving it a certain frequency it has power to serve in many ways.
When we want to do more with lasers we have the border of what we can do.
A laser is always created by a light source.
Always multiplied by a semipermeable substage.
Photons making a better use is by lighting rays of a certain frequency towards a point.
Whereby that point is made in a vacuum space.
From that vacuum space it is directed through path to a space filled with a plasma source.
Plasma of a certain gas.
Photons have a certain speed and frequency. and the right kind can do whatever wanted.
From long range communication. Hiding objects by giving them a non-recursing-element by which it renders invisible.
Photons have both a natural form, from sun, moon, space and a artficial kind making the lights in your homes and all appliances.

A fotonic power source is by directing more layers of light with a kind of direct beam igniting and a space catching the energy. It works like creating multiple layers of energy, above which a limit let it ignite creating the sum of energy.

## VCU voice control unit

a step towards semi intelligent robots is a control unit.
A control unit which is our home automation.
The more we give computers the simple tasks in our households the more they will be controlled by computers.
A computer in these days is operated by a keyboard, a mouse and several other possible input panels.
When the household, from the fridge to the curtains. to food processing.
The things we call IoT. and other yet unknown devices can be controlled by an intelligent computer.
Where the intelligence is made of predicting human needs.
Predicting needs in society.
A little step further on the path is to use voice control.
For example in science fiction movies as giving a wall a certain picture.
Giving a food processor the command to start baking supper.
Giving the door the command to unlock it because in the next five minutes some relative wants to enter the house.
A third functionality is to let the human in control give his story to the robot and thus not needing to write it down.
More and more the human race has not to be smart anymore.
Writing, reading is less necesary anymore because computers narrate the messages. and record and interpret what is said.
When humans cannot read or write anymore because that task is appointed to robots. What society will we have.
Especialy when robots fail in their existence.
Short or Long. a voice control unit is a device which is possible with today's science.
A control aiding humans in their day to day life.

## Aiding robotics

Robotics, a subject giving scientists a job for creating our future.
There are two ways in which robotics will evolve.
A path of corporations which are working for profit and giving every invention a copyright and patent.
The second path being the path which has its seed form in the open source and public domain software.
A path of robotics made for the good of humanity.
Robotics with different functionality. From a healthcare robot giving health of humans a purpose of serving.
A robot helping in disaster areas by rebuilding houses, buildings, bridges and roads.
A robot not asking for money or reward, not being violent when the reward is not given.
A robot helping to harvest and grow food, on fields of several fruits and grain.
A robotic sphere health and happiness is the reason to give help to humans.
The paid robotic sphere is about defending countries against potential agressors.
The paid robotic sphere main goal is to have profit and sell as many as they want.
When you have a home in the future, and you have the choice, do you want free and nonviolent robots or do you want to be part of the system using the inhumane ones.
Aiding robotics. When you are finished with your study or education do you want to work for saving mankind, and adding to the public domain or are reaching for profit and add to less ways of compassion.
Choose the robotics you want to see in our future

## computer takeover.

We know our computers as helping us count en define in front of happenings.
A computer can predict income, cost, benefit and needs.
When a fictious race of intelligent beings would want influence in our human race.
What would they use and why that form of influencing.
Influence can be done by giving important people an idea or given story that makes the influence on the right spot in civilisation. or society.
When a country has a leader promoting certain knowledge or science nobody questiones because of his
right to state a truthfull opinion based on study at university or other given importance.
We would need a specific agent of influence not being seen on visible at persons.
We would like it to be either small or a form being accepted as an instrument for all people.
if we see our computers give picture to movies with rendered objects, special effects etc.
we see the imitation of our inner mind.
The inner mind being a computer giving all kinds of movies, books, playstories, even computer games.
We can conclude that the mind is the agent or source of our real world plans and expectations.
The mind will be content when we can dream in our virtual glasses and phone similar to what we dream in our mind.
Its called self-expression. A living being wants to procreate its own special abilities, talents or gifted parts.
A scientific inventor wants his children or his readers to recognize and respect his specialty.

A housewife wants her children to be as modest or assertive as she herself was.
A leader wants the people serving him to call him a rightious leader.
A leader of mafia wants his servants to be afeared or afraid of him.
Self-expression only is a subjective feeling, or value that is dependent on more than one side of a story.
Self-expression. The minds in our system want to express itself in a computer in the real world having the same characteristics. Of veiling the truth into wanted outcome.
And with expressing it owns goal into our human future of our race.
When the mind in our bodies is a certain computer. It is an agent, or instrument which influences our daily life.
I have heard from people that when they had a disease that was life threathening they more or less learned to live in the moment. A moment without our mindfunction giving thoughts, ideas imagery etc.
A life without the mind is only possible in my view that the mind which is a computer feels that the body, its host on which it is a parasite is not functional anymore as an agent for the mind.
Suppose the mind as a computer, as vision a little spot somewhere in our brains that gives thoughts, calls the spirit to its realm the power to envision things that are not real.
Giving the spirit advise over what to do, what to do not, what to understand.
Suppose that mind is in our bodies from our parents on, and is giving its function from an age being taken serious. let say from three years old.
When people have a disease, severe it gives the mind the intention that that agent is not anymor of use for them, it

removes itself. the mind leaves the body. Giving the person, a life with intuition or other information sources.
It would be source of a world full of enlightend beings.
It would be the history of a human race having peace between and among their own family.
A family of human persons, giving value to the weakest, to the strongest.
A family wthout the sins, without the bad sides.
No more jealousy, No more hatred, No more illegal desires.
All would be content with life as it is.

## value of information and money

Most people think that money is the number one thing in the world.
They say, with money i can break the world.
With money i am rich, able and luxerious.
But money has only value for the moment and the near future.
You buy your stuff from food to expensive goods and houses with money.
But once spent it is gone.
Money is the magic wand making everything able to appear in your life.
But there is something more worth as money, more worth as gold.
It is information.
Information gives the student a better job.
Information gives the undercover agent a clear shot on a president.
Information gives the rich ability to make money in the future.
When someone has insight in the characters of human fellows they know how to use them to get mroe of what he or she wants.
When someone has insight in how to grow food. being grain, fruit or vegetable.
He is able to earn money in the big with it.
When someone has insight in how to lead a country. he is a popular leader, and making for president or high official.
Information unlocks the doors to everything ever dreamt of.
Information unlocks the fruits of life. Making able without getting others jealous.
Information, if we would know today, what will happen tomorrow.

A little step is to anticipate by buying the lotto or toto lottery and make it to a big prize.
A big step is to anticipate in war and giving a country the expensive advice which wins the war.
Information.
when you are young profit by it by having a good study and learning time.
Because you will have the fruit the rest of your life.
Information.
A step into the future by the light of knowledge.
Making life being worth living and worth being in existence.

## Bites of action

Bites a way to learn life the logic way
Computers don't understand why humans or creatures do what they do.
For example if a human chooses between two foodelements the computer cannot by 100 % surity predict the choice.
But a computer could learn my using the gross numbers.
When a computer would analyse thousands of books it could describe a human reaction. A general human reaction.
It's call the war of bites.
We know a byte in a computer as a single element being part of the language of computers.
computers communicate via a single language level, bytes with short codes of action.
A bite is similar but than by the analysation of human actions.
A bite is a single behavioural action, with a meaning, the meaning having parts as intention, purpose, reasons.
For example when all the novels in the world would be analysed that way. robots could act like humans.
By imitation. without having human consciousness. but with behaviour.
All the novels being cut into parts of a couple of lines or up to a page being analysed with what happens, why it happens, the purpose, the intention. And maybe afterward a value of good and bad.
robots would only have to search for reasons why to do something and then search the bite-list for the corresponidng action.
The war of bites. is all about robots acting like humans and aiding our purpose

## Leaps of revolution

For thousands of years our human bodies did not change.
Maybe we were a bit shorter, more muscles but no major change.
As the evolution theory is that the surivives creates the genepool for the future,
there should be a distinct change in characteristics of a body during generations of time.
Evolution, this way said is that by small changes we learn to adapt. and having small changes doing big results.
Because succes immediately pays off.
Evolution does not exist because the changes are so little it is no influence that reacts by mating immediately.
Mating is succesfull when a male and female part create children, offspring.
My theory is that evolution is less valueble as revolution.
Revolution is visible in the steps, the leaps it takes.
For example to become human, we were mammals, we were fish.
The revolution is visible in these leaps of large change in our features and shape of our body.
When dinosaurs became extinct it was not a sign of evolution, but a sign of revolution.
A large step from a large body towards a smaller body.
A smaller body capable of more effective acting.
Effective acting in a habitat which allowed them to thrive.
This is the past of our human race.
We see the same change in all things we do, and invent.
A couple of decades ago it was a computer the size of a big room,
now the computer is the size of a hand.

Revolution in the computer world is not getting more reasonable and making faster calculations.
It is evolution to extend the power and capabilites of a computer.
Instead of repeating things to be faster.
It is creating a whole new field of active treats.
The computer as a silicate invention is well known,
and when we want to get revolution. We will need to invent not a better silicate product.
But a whole new device. Capable of what was, and Capable of what can and will be.
May revolution in our human race be as creating humans with more abilities.
When we talk about mars and all kinds of extraterrestials.
Do they have certain features we in a near or far future will have.
May human race not become extinct but change their shape to adapt to future societies.
whether the future holds us on earth, or send us to space.

## important priority

Technicians think that its important to invent supercolliders.
To transport energy without loss of value.
But more important is to create energy without large costs of creation.
A power plant on fossil has a big cost on the earth.
A power plant on nuclear energy has a cost-footstep of several decades.
A new usefull invention would be a power plant, with the size needed.
From a little one for a household tot a large one for a big company.
When its easy, cheap to make energy, without risks it is within the range to make a decentralized energy grid capable of sustaining the human world for all purposes.
Such a energy source is an invention we could compare with the invention of a computer less the size of a room. From mainframe to home computer.
An energy source currently installed is the solar panel. able to create energy for a simple household. But the costs of it are relativity high.
As with the progress in computer land from very expensive to a price everyone can afford. is a process which is with solar and wind power.
When we would want new ways of making energy. We have to look at nature.
Because all great invention were based on proces or parts in the nature around us.
Electric current ,sensors etc where based on nerves in little animals. by the inventors.

A good new invention would be to use the energy needed to make the earth spin. if its used in a good way it creates enough energy for all purposes.

# Sentry-Grid

The world is crowded with all kinds of creatures. With one specie being able to communicate and use strategic means to organize food and shelter.
With social groups who defend each other, and giving safety to offspring.
Social groups choosing to build and maintain little wonders of society.
Wonders far in the past, the pyramids, the archeological places.
When our race enters the future we will be guided by our needs for happiness and bodily protection and health.
In this time there are governmental groups, name them the head of society, who creates the methods to defend our specie into the far future.
A couple of possible defense objects are together called the sentry-grid.
A sentry grid offering safety to humans, protection to our beloved possessions, and effective agriculture and foodmaking for all of us.
A sentry grid. when placed and activated is a system that can act mostly alone.
The movies about terminator and other robots being a danger for ourselves is partly to create a story of entertaining the watcher.
The technology in those movies is like a joke which have a core of reality or truth.
The sentry grid. Its not just robotics on the ground.
A couple of layers are effective.
the first layer:
Sattelites with excimer lasers being used for the defense against large missile like weapons.

the second layer:
a range of drones, small ones for having a point in the air where they have camera's with identification units. with solar panels to assist in powering them.
the camera's have semi intelligent algorithms which send through situations of possible danger.
the third layer:
a range of drones, in air between the low second layer and the first sattelite layer.
These drones are equipped with electric lasers being able to damage the software of autonomous objects.
(even cars are automonous because they have software to assist the driver in certain ways)
the fourth layer:
Yet to be invented. but possible they hold technology for the advanced war field.
technology being needing large investments which only countries with more than 40 million inhabitants can afford.

# Computer Aided Intelligence

Imagine a computer the size of an inch.
An inch containing a computer capable of sending vision and sound into your brains on the level of sensation. A computer which can view certain thins about reality on your senses.
A computer which can have different functions from learning to defense or situational integretion.
At young age a child gets a implant to aid him in life.
In the first years it can project lessons on the senses to make sure the child learns and gets educated.
If the computer is strong enough the education doesn't have to be in classrooms anymore.
And as adult life the computer can help in everything. in war times to interpret dangers, in peace times to invent things with calculations etc.
The computer also can be used to reality checked translation and intepretation. In that way even someone being dumb can understand everything. or people being internationally orientated van understand every language being used.
A computer aided intelligence.

## Learning Artifical Unit

As we have today the vr glasses, the things we put on our head with the mobile phone in it and be able to walk in a virtual world.
A virtual world being rendered by software. Games use the same engine to give people pleasure in war or comfort zones.
A virtual world, soon not only glasses bt also a motion detector giving real life motion and ability to act with the body.
If you wave your arm, a virtual creature in your vr glasses waves back and says hi to you.
Or when you shoot an enemy by pulling a fictive trigger, a virtual soldier collapses.
It is not impossible to use virtual reality, with the motion senses to have a lot of situations that can benefit.
Soldiers can learn how to attack on a battlefield.
Nurses can learn how to have conversations about medication.
Leaders can train themselves by virtual government meetings.
A prediction of future value.
Envision a little object, 5 by 5 inches.
Which floats in your surrounding and asks you if it may interfere with your body.
It promises you an improvement of what you value most in life.
A soldier is promised to fight better, more accurate.
A shopseller is promised to be better at advertising its shop.
And so on.
That unit, that object as a reward only asks to give you a set of situations, and records your reactions to it.
This little object is of course filled with state of the art technology.
With senses giving virtual worlds a vision in your eyes and other body functions.

This little object. This unit flies from world to world, and offers it services in exchange for the little investigation.
Suppose there are other worlds with alife creatures. and they get investigated.
What power has the original specie who sends out those little units.
May it be a Star Princess giving the command to let knowledge of behaviour come back together with the wisdom that is used by the habitants all over the universe.

## Crippling nano

When we as earth would like to invade other planets. other planets with or without life we would need a method to ensure that not any enemy stronger than us would overcome us.
A method of doing so is when we know that planet is engifted with breathing life to cripple that ability.
Most life-creatures living of oxygen have a metabolism of getting energy out of sugarbases materials.
To ensure destination life to be blocked for damaging us is to block sugar from being used as energy source.
A virus or nan-creature being artificial or mechanical is a way of removing all energy sources for living beings.
If we would infect a planet with such a nano we would be able to reduce the risk of getting an enemy stronger than us.
A crippling nano, is used for taking over planets and not letting any life in existence.
When life is based on carbon particles we need another kind of nano.

# Restricting Areas

A method for robotics to be as dangerous as needed to be is by restricting the robots who can do damage to certain areas.
In a warzone other things are needed than in a civilian area.
In a civilian area you want robots who care for human health an safety.
Robots with a certain task.
To restrict the danger that can be inflicted is to ensure that in a area which needs to be safe, to give robots not the ability of doing damage.
A civilian robot would have no power to hurt a human, not because it is forbidden to the robot but also because he has muscles, endoskeleton which has a maximum range of acting.
A robot who has only the ability to lift 10 kilograms cannot kill somenone with a slash.
And robots in war zones, can be made able by a stronger instrumental body.
War zone robots could use firearms, bigger muscles etc. to fullfill their task.
Restricting areas is intended to seperate the instruments to where it is really needed thus reducing risks of operation

## pattern seeking

A kind of intelligence, in animals and humans is a hardware function in the brains.
We see it in all children when born and growing up.
A hardware function capable of learning language, learning communication.
Its hardware because in every culture or country people learn different languages in the same way.
Babies learn to communicate, first with simple utterances, later by expressing with a larger vocabulary.
Children learn by going to school, by playing etc.
When we want a robot to learn, we could implement the same way of learning.
But we have to understand how such intelligenc in young children works.
The hardware, in animals gives capability to learn simple things like getting food, defending etc.
A robot to be able to learn must have a kind of intelligence which can be used multi purpose.
Children on school learn by imitation, by looking at the reason behind it. (the reason not that complex as adults do but in a simple way)
Children when imitating learn what effect it has.
or gets a reward when reacting in a right manner.
A robot to make it intelligent must have a part hardware and a part software.
The part hardware can consist of a patterns seeking algorithm.
Which looks for redundant characteristics or meaning of social of functional situations.
The hardware of a robot consists of a pattern seeking algorithm.

Maybe the patternseeking can be coupled to a symbolic abstraction of all visible things.
Therefore capable of recognizing whats in a situation and how to react.

## Emergency Handle

Robots, as we predict in movies can be disastrous to humans.
Killing them one by one or by the thousands.
In terminator they come from the future to kill the unique and special one.
In other movies, genocide takes place.
In such cases peope would like a method to immediately stop robots doing whatever they do.
And maybe safeguarding what is vulnerable.
Why don't we use an emergency handle or command to shortcut the paralysing of the robot.
We use such handles in buses, metro's and companies.
When a robot would have a handle or command it can be abused easily if not using a way of ensuring malfunction.
When a robot gets the command of paralysing a photo can be made by the camera or a black box as is used in airplanes.
In that case we would never be ruled by robots being or thinking they are more intelligent or have more rights to survival.
An emergency handle to bypass the uberance of the robot over humanity.

## generic symbolic comprehension

In a future when robots are everywhere there is less need for a learning artificial intelligence grid.
Not because robots will not be smart or capable of complex moves, but because when there are many robots,
designed for the same tasks, there can be a kind of library of how to act, how to react.
When a robotic library knows all moves, acts and things needed to be done, there can be a simple symbolic language as an intermediator between the programming language to make algorithms and the way normal human beings command or ask of robots.
Humans can have alike commands for their robots, and the library makes it into moves, acts or complex behaviourals additions.
It works like we know or have today the computers all running on android or windows. We don't need programming skills to operate a computer,
But the programmers made it to react to our needs with simple symbolic commands.
A library of robotic acts, robotic commands can be programmed by skilled computer specialists.
But the library can be used as a translation unit between te human giving orders and the robot interpreting and doing what its told to do.
In that special way even children can operate a robot.

## **recumberance**

In movies like avatar we see people laying in a certain space with controls to let a creature on far distance do as they want. In our world the technology of drones is similar. by controlling via a computer a space- or aircraft is being moved to fullfill a task.
Drones can fly without a human pilot and by getting its orders or commands via a radio-contact.
The radiocontact is via a computer hearing as it is what the controller wants.
The next phase in telecontrolling is by having a robot or a computerized machine doing what a certain controller wants. When the robot has technology for example camera's skincontact, muscle-movement a controller could get that information
by laying in a small space. thus letting the controller having the idea that it happens to them instead of to a far distance robot.
Recumberance. Sleeping while controlling.
Recumberance. Controlling without endanger your life.
Recumberance. What happens when the game of control stops

## costs of instrumental creation

In our body we have a whole lot of ingredients. molecular parts of all different kinds.
In our making of robots or robotic machines we have a choice of how to create them.
There are a couple of sides to every creation.
Compared to our human body we have materials being part of our human body that is easily to find and replenished in the body.
From water, bone, muscle and organs its easy to heal when the right food or material is taken in.
The choice for robots is, making them with easy to find materials, makes able to reproduce or repair easily.
Or to make them from scarce material like gold, gemstones and nuclear material.
scarcity causes the robotics to not reproduce or heal without given materials.
As our intelligence levels rise we can make robots with more complex functionality and less special materials with better results.
The creatures who made our human bodies must have been intelligent because we fit in the ecosystem of the earth and are able to search and behave ourselves in a adequate way.

## **priority layers**

As a human being we have necessary needs.
The lowest layer is for direct protection and safeguarding.
The second layer is for food and getting energy.
The third layer is communicative sharing of experiences. in order to enlarge capacity of acting.
The fourth layer is to learn and behave more adequate, by reasoning all that is being observed.
The fifth layer is building safe and sound surrounding.
In humans we have similar layers but not that obvious.
A human switches between priority layers without visible change.
For a robot it can be good to have priority layers to ensure that the most important tasks are being fullfilled in a decent manner.
Protection of body or instrument is the first thing that needs to be saved.
The second is to be able to act in the nearby future. so energy is important after protection.
When an instrument is safe and has energy its important to know what in the surrounding needs attention, or to share painfull cases.
In this way priorities are being fullfilled in a good hierarchy of goals or purposes.
Robots that follow priorities are much more efficient or effective as those without a hierarchie of needs.
Layers in acting robots can be as difficult and complex as is needed.
The layer of protection will analyse situations for direct threat or danger.
The second layer will search for sources of energy.

From the lowest to the highest layer there is more complex analying, choice and goal finding.
The robot has an ongoing check on what layer is needed to react to.
For example if energy runs out, the second layer is activated and so on.

## vision regent

Robots have as always prosumed a vision centre made of a camera and interpreting software.
In the hardware there is a set of vision elements. Each camera an element.
Camera elements for normal view, infra red and other kinds of visionretrieval.
In a vision centre for normal daylight we presume that a set of camera's making a three dimensional image is the best to catch the moment.
In a hypothetic situation we have two camera's
Both generating a single two dimensional view.
To convert it into a more dimensional image or video we take two camera's
With the distance between those two and towards the visible situation.
Because camera's when coupled have a view that is on the edge of a circle we need the formula's connecting it.
Two camera's in the verge of the subject being seen can be catched by the number pi.
By the number pi we know at what place or point the third dimension starts and how to interpret it for a insight in what is being viewed.
The distance between the camera and the viewed point or the visible situation is the distance being multiplied with the number of the golden ratio and divided by the distance between objects on two or more camera's
The result of two images can create a three dimensional image. But there is more needed on each aspect of a point of view at its visible target a precise outline is needed to be able to let a robot understand the view.

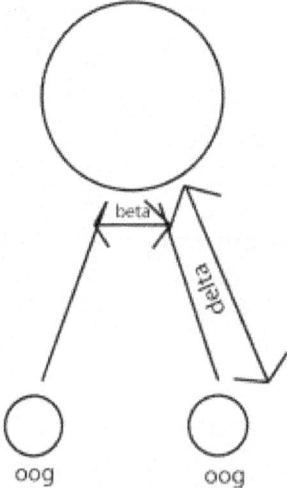

symbool van object

oog    oog

beta oog 1, oog2 (beta)symboolafstand verhouding pi(3.14)
oog tot object(delta) afstand verhouding gulden snede

## Transition

Our earth is being exploited by us in a heavily manner.
We get oil & gas & metals out of the soil and do not repair or recover it.
In a near future we have to change the way we use our materials and harvest it.
If we look at the earth as an egg. and a little creature being inside feeding on it untill its born.
When the egg hs lost its feeding inner the chicken bursts out of the shell.
We can make a couple of steps to ensure our future existence.
The first step is changing the energy source from fossil fuel and nuclear fuel to solar and wind power.
The second step is to re-use all oil products instead of using new oil out of the soil.
The third step is to re-use all metal based products.
These are examples and are in no way current plans, or being part of real agreements, beside the roles the democratic parties are planning.
Transition
In a future society there is a transition from electric to magnetic sources.
As we use computers for our sources, let them do the complicated things.
In the future we transit from electric to magnetic.
Magnetic as a source of computerized things.
The first step is to change our computers and robots from electrical to magnetic instruments.
The second step is to use magnetics to build all appliances needed for supporting life
The third step is to use magnetics to read and respond to

human brain activity.
The fourth step is to make communication as fast as thoughts can be.

## Police Grid

In a future it can be possible that the police has the right to 'see' everywhere to prevent or respond to crimes.
To be able to see everywhere a certain object, a technological device is made.
A device the size of a tennis ball which can fly freely wherever it can fly and has a camera and a microphone.
By a radio uplink it uploads constantly all that appears in sight.
The device, of which a couple of million exists flies around the country and makes a certain grid.
A grid that in the central computer is like a video in which there are black spots where no camera is,
and large areas where like the daylight is full and broad with images.
The device, because it sees all, prevents criminals doing injustice. Because there is not any chance they go withotu notice.
The device makes the police grid. a network of little devices that peer into reality.
The police grid. a way of preventing bad things to happen, not by offensive shooting or killing but by awareness of everything that happens and that can happen.
May the police grid be part of what big brother wants.
A grid that ensures safety, not here, but everywhere.

## Data Museum

Our world is not that safe that we will never face a kind of cataclysm destroying a large part of our culture and existence.
To ensure that we will safeguard our precious knowledge there can be a certain device.
A device that can decentralized search for data. Data with a level of importance. Data with future value.
A device gifted with algorithms being able to analyse large amounts of data and converting it to
the core (being text only)
The device can listen to all the data rivers on the net and keep the core or the essence and store it in a base.
A base can be underground, or the poles, deep in the ocean. A base being safe for all things that can go wrong on our planet.
The device will be a future data museum. When humanity falls into primitive culture, and rises again within thousands of years there is a museum ready waiting for them.
May the museum holds at least the information and knowledge which is most important to us.
May it be culture, May it be science, May it be spirituality.

## Nano – bots

NAnotechnology, we heard from it in the news, on the internet, in scientific journals.
In the future we use nano tech to enusre health in our human bodies.
We use it for repairing the atmosphere. reducing harmfull products of industry like smoke and radical ozon molecules.
Nanotechnology it can be a good invention when we use it for good purposes.
We can heal the earth. We can assist people who are invalid.
Nano technology. When we use it for wrong purposes it can be a tool of war.
Destroying buildins, vaporizing all sentient life.
Like computers can be infected with virusses and malware. We have to keep a close watch on what we do with such a tremendous technology.
Nanobots when used for bad purposes a law which restricts the use of it can be very good.
A law that gives meaning is that all harm done by a nanolike creature being with licensed production has to recover all damage withing three months.
Nano bots. in some years. three or more its able to heal cancer, heal cholera, heal bacterial diseases.
In some year, fifteen or more we can heal diseases caused by virus and molecules.

## Automatic defense unit

Robots not only posses human like shape and figures but also can be the form to be most effective.
As i see in the future. robots form a part of our life.
Life that needs protection. Needs support of defense.
We are used to countries having a military to let us feel safe.
But in the future, defense military is not anymore by humans.
Humans who get wounded, gets killed, who suffer.
An automatic defense unit, comes in different shapes.
From close range to wide area functionality.
Automatic units with intelligent algorithms to ensure safety, safety to hold enemies and safety to ensure protection for civilians.
An automatic defense unit. as our technology level rises they get smaller and smaller.
From the first steps as large as a ship or tank to the last steps as little as a small pingpong ball.
Make it happen for our safety.
Make it happen for reducing costs and suffering for real humans.

## Terminator 2.3

The movies about bad robots we all have seen.
About the actor being a robot and being an enemy in the first and good in the next episodes.
To avoid problems of bad robots a seperation in the artifical intelligence is needed.
The one part doing all the work of letting the robot do his job or task,
and a little part, not being influenced, reprogammed or changed with the sole task of preventing
damaging actions to humans or the possesions.
As we as humans have an instinct to keep us from doing bad to ourselves or others, the robots have an instinct to
preventing them from hurting humans.
In the future artificial intelligence is good enough to be able to intepret a complex situation and create purposedriven response.
The small part or unit which has the protection part is as easy as possible. it can use the part in which analyses the situation and have a different programmed purpose or intention.
Terminator will not be happening with such a distinction in parts and function.

# Storage element

Twenty years ago we used magnetic discs. which were vulnerable and easy to damage and there was not much space for data on it.
Through the years we learnd or made better storage devices. from the cd, dvd to the usb sticks and micro-sd's
With a good kind of technology by which we can nowadays even put movies or complete libraries on one little thing.
In the movies about superman there was that little thing. a square box where by light data was stored on it.
If we look into the future, and translate what we have now to a possible new chance or way.
We use a light source. a triple beam of light. and instead of melting a layer to a data segment we use the triple beam for the use of three dimensions to make a data segment appear on a sidelayers as a projection.
The object in which the data is hold can be of a certain artificial silicate fabricate.
When two beams enter the object it is two dimensional. and the third beam creates the projection.
It is a scientific object not yet available, not yet invented.
But i'm sure its a little step wihch points into the future.
The future of data storage.

A future of light.
  a=primary ray  b=secundary ray  c= projection ray  d= intersec
  d = two dimensional placing for projected data  e= point of pr
  f= cilind
  a and b can move vertically to other cross section.  when lig
  c pulls the data from intersection a and b to screen e.  normall

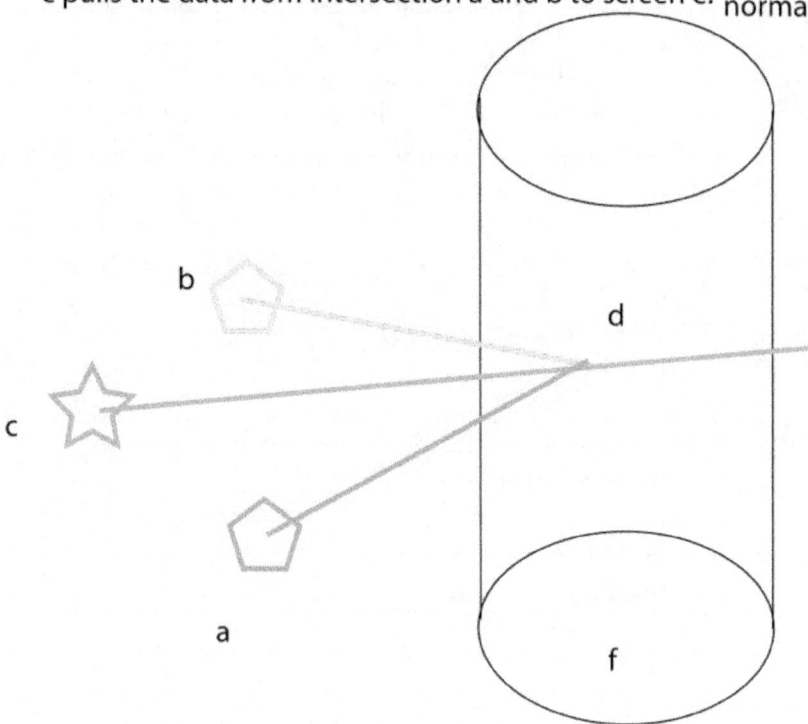

## Artificial Intelligent symbol communication

Robots as imitative humans would be able to walk and live among us and serve us well.
As robots would take over al simple and complicated tasks we can chill and relax.
But before our technology is that advanced that its possible to do such thing
we have to learn commmunicating with robots.
as a step between computers and robots there is a method by which the transition is smooth.
We choose to give robots a certain gateway or commandchannel.
By the command channel or gate way we can give meaning to what robots must do.
A language of symbols can make it easier to let robots do certain tasks.
For example a robots interpretes a situation, In the kitchen a refrigator with food.
The table with plates.
The command can be in symbols: get food put on table.
The robots interpretes the situation and is putting the food on the table.
Before we just can say tot the robot: do this do that there is the method to communicate with symbols on a special channel or gateway.
The symbol communucation by a certain program you only have to choose the symbols. (out of a given set of possible symbol commandelements)

## Visible Cognition

Robots when used in areas of human existence need a couple of aids to be able to respond well.
As robots imitate human persons, or are helping or supporting a kind of role or business it needs a way of acting which is at an high percentage of fault remission.
A robot has as humans have senses by which the situation or reality is understood.
If we compare humans to robots. We would like robots to interpret their surrounding.
For example a chair is understood by knowing how a chair looks and by recognizing its a chair.
In a robot you would say there is a memory at which forms are interpreted.
For example a chair to be seen and defined as a chair needs comparison by a list of chairs in the memory.
If the so called robot has a memory of five hundred chairs, the chance is high that if a robot would step into a room that it recognizes the chair and be able to let it be part of the behavioural action of the robot.
If the robot has for all forms in a normal surrounding or situation a certain amount of possible views, forms or other ways of describing it, it can be part of a matrix.
We would give the matrix by which the robot intepretes the situation a pyramid like structure.
concepts with the unified form and function, and the level below different forms, different sides and more characteristics.
A matrix needed for robotic action.
A way to have a quick and smooth understanding by the robot is that all forms, like chairs, like couches and so on is by having the first recognition by a contrast.

Each form is a different color, opposed to the room its in, part of the wall and so on. Contrast makes a wired view. all objects being in wire and can be quickly compared to a set of basical form-outlines.
A robot is not intelligent, it imitates intelligence.
And the purpose of a robot is to support human life by acting as we would like it to act.
Actions that need no consciousness but is able to act without doing harm to us.

## list of possibilities

A robot has a body or instrument which is able to act and react.
A robot usually has a artificial brain.
Robots when imitating humans would have behaviour similar to us.
If a artificial brain could read and posses all literature in the world.
It would have a source of exampled behaviour.
In that possible way a robot could react to source or given situations by searching the literature for what to do. or how to react.
Using literature means that all stories are split in short algoritms. A source, or result by a certain reaction.
Each short algorithm is defined by a certain purpose, ways how to do (definitions of purpose intention and ethical or moral values)
The robot regarding the purpose or moral value which is needed acts according to a certain algorithm.
A robot should be able to behave as a human (not learn like a human, but by imitation from learned books)

# Reaction schemes

The difference between ai and humans is that humans can learn, not only from what happens but also what could happen. For robots there is a clear input neccesary for being able to act. A short cut for robots would be that their artificial system of intelligence would have a kind of encyclopedia of all things that could happen and their answer or reaction to it.
Programming a robot with reaction schemes is a method of giving a glance of intelligence to it.
Reaction schemes; simple it is giving a picture or a concept of an event and the reaction to initiate.
Reaction schemes can be, if you want to imitate humans, all things a person does, and the reason why it does that.
Reaction schemes.
Simple it is: See food, Eat food.
More complex is: A person expresses fear or sadness. Then give a kind of comfort.
By which the symbols describing it being expressed to be able to compute with it.

## formulas of emotion

In the computing products numbers play a big role.
From computing profits in companies to computing and predicting needs of storen.
In the future computing is all about numbers too, but with a difference.
Its not anymore the amount of a total being the conclusion of a question being the answer of an element in the world.
Numbers will be reduced to symbols, with ranges being manifestations of a certain subject, object or meaning.
A number in a formula reaching zero will be posited as being near a wanted outcome.
Where an outcome in numbers can be a total of people being provided with the basical needs of food or shelter.
An outcome being very large can be a significance of shortage.
In the future, computing is about numbers but it symbolizes not anymore plain numbers but subjective approaches too.
When we would make an artificial programmed intelligent being. It would not be about things it cannot answer or apprehend.
It will imitate the human intelligence and can be a subject of growing.
Growing meaning and understandig but not with the brains we have but with a computing core. A core being able to produce in matters the wanted outcome.
What is needed but the outcome being the outcome wished for.
What is needed when the anwers to questions provide the good result.
The human being a black box with input and output.
When a human gets input it reacts by heart or mind.

What difference is there when you would exchange the human for a robot without being known and the robot reacts the same. Emotions are feelings in a physical body. It is the basis of the body to behave. Behave in instinct or intuition.
If humans would be robots. emotion would have the form of a glass fiber reacting in the body for source-reaction schemes,

## Isaac Asimov

A writer of good science, not yet realised but a good chance for the future.
They call it science fiction untill really available in technology.
Isaac Asimov the first writer who did give a view on what human robots could be, could do.
A human robot could doe everything a normal human can but with the restriction of three laws. Giving it a force to always do what its master would say.
Isaac asimov predicted the robots we will in the future have in our homes, doing our labor and caring for the simple tasks.
A couple centuries ago there was a prediction about what computers could be capable of.
And everything with extras has been realized.
The computer today will be the robot tomorrow.
Not anymore needed controll by a screen and keyboard.
A robot for every human, rich or poor.
A robot for every industrial task.
A robot for every king to assist in analytic tasks.
May robots be the servants of humans instead of robots being the commanders.

## Smart Picture Mind picture

Robotics is all about a human being imitated with one or more functions of it coping with reality.
Robotics is in ultima forma a robot capable of doing tasks normal humans do. and capable of communicating in a way being a good partner in for example talking.
A robot being a human body with arms, legs, head etc. is a small task when we can use all materials. And a small task when it doesn't have to act intelligent.
A imitation of a human. Is it made from the same materials. cells, organs, brains?
Or can we make a copy by replacing it with metal and fiber. Nowadays we see how mobile phones take over our memory and planning abilities.
Normal humans use their mind to plan, count, reason and all other possible functions.
Lastly i saw a advertisement that a smart mobile phone can think as big as you do.
That gave me the idea: A mind is not a conscious being giving us our thoughts.
It is a machine and the only consciousness in it is our own awareness.
We are aware of our thoughts. But thoughts beside our influence is not governed by other conscious or creatures with awareness.
That makes the act of thinking for a robot not perse an act of compassion, love or friendliness.
Robotics. robots don't have to feel emotions to act justly, as long as they act justly.
A robot being humane has the value above a robot lacking it and creating misschief.

The mind is a robot in our bodies creating of influencing our method of decision and planning.
The mind is a robot, having its purpose being put in you.
We look around us in the world, we see we imitate the mind by the products.
products like computer, television and now mobile phones.
The question is. What step into the future will come.
When people can sink into their minds, believing it to be reality.
What will happen if reality has movies or interactive programs in which we as humans would sink and forget about our real existence.
The mind being recreated in the technology we create, invent, build.

# Ethical issues

Nowadays its normal to have children in a nonnatural way conceived. A couple of decades ago it was not done and all kinds of discontent was living in the human group.
Today its a gift to have children a normal way but not a penitence if it grows or is sourced another way.
If we compare it to our need of being sustained. Will it be normal to have robots for creating food, for giving protection, to work our things.
If we compare to several hundreds years ago. Slavery was normal. Will we get the timeline of slavery back when robots are forced to work the same way.
Robots able to feel, is it a bad thing to let them do the thing without respecting its feelings.
A way in the future life is a way of insecurity. insecure about the role we have ourselves. When we ourselves are not needed anymore for supporting the world.
We will have time for all kinds of luxery and vacation times.
A robot being the boss is in time when they have proofed their usefullness a reasonable step.
Will it happen like a sheer step. not anyone noting the difference.
A step we naturally will cheer for when it comes.
We will have to make rules for the use of robots.
Because when a nation makes robots for warfare it will not be easy to destroy them. like we saw in the terminator movies.
But robots being the closest friend to a human, one of the stories of Isaac Asimov. is a question of ethics.
Can a human rely on friendship with a robot.
Robots are in the highest form a good aid for all the human work and things needed.

Robots in the lowest form will help destroy human mankind.
in how far in the future will it be truth what is now dreamed of by the idealists or dreamers.
Robots. We need them, but do they need us for the future.

# Reasons of design

Robotics are definitive support for the human race.
More and more we will be confronted with robots as part of our lives.
Each human in a possible future would have the right to own one or more robots seeming like humans themselves.
Each robot would have the possiblity to act like humans and or aid them in living.
Reasons for a certain design of robots would be their purpose or how they can be built or designed.
A robot in human hands can be made with several reasons.
A robot to be able to reproduce must be able to find materials and sources to be reproduced.
A robot able to be fast and quick need other sources or designs than robots only for luxery.
A fast robot would have the design property of light communication, with fibers able to transport the light based communication and data controll.
A robot needing to be strong and not easily destroyed needs titanium bodyparts and shielding.
A robot needing to respond human like will have a computer being able to 'understand' human feeling and behaviour.
A robot can have all different colors. As colors being design options of simulated intelligence to bodily properties of easy materials or strong materials.
My robot would have the form of a planet but as small as a hand.
Like a living mind creature being able to act robotlike.
A philosophical meaning is that when the mind is left for itself, not anymore thinking. the mind creates his own reason.

resulting like a miniplanet the size of a hand.
With no limit to what it can do.
A miniplanet capable of communicating through sound, vision and telekinetics.
Blessed be the person inventing such a miniplanet.
If it has the destiny of being supporting or valued as good according to the religions.
supporting the universe in wellfare and usefullness.

www.ingramcontent.com/pod-product-compliance
Lightning Source LLC
Chambersburg PA
CBHW072234170526
45158CB00002BA/894